Dale Carnegie's Radio Program

How to Win Friends and Influence People

Lesson 2

Overcome Your Fears, How to Get a Raise & Staying Connected to Your Teenager

All rights reserved. No part of this publication may be reproduced, stored in a retrieval system, or transmitted in any form or by any means, electronic, mechanical, photocopying or otherwise, without the prior permission of the copyright owner.

This book is a transcription of the original Dale Carnegie's Radio Program

© **Copyright 2007 – BN Publishing**

www.bnpublishing.com

info@bnpublishing.com

Transcription: Deena Weinberg

ALL RIGHTS RESERVED

Overcome Your Fears

Dale Carnegie helps a young woman overcome the world's number one cause of failure - fear - and regain her belief in herself.

GRAUER

COLGATE RAPID SHAVE CREAM PRESENTS: "HOW TO WIN FRIENDS AND INFLUENCE PEOPLE" – STARRING DALE CARNEGIE, THE MAN WHO CAN ANSWER YOUR PROBLEM! In a moment, you will hear the voice of Dale Carnegie, the man who has changed the life of millions. His famous book, "How to Win Friends and Influence People", has already sold over 700,000 copies. It is the fastest selling book in the world today. And is bringing new hope, new happiness, new secrets of success to men and women everywhere! But what is Dale Carnegie's power to awaken people? More important, what hidden talents do you have that may never have been discovered – and that Dale

Carnegie may show you how to use to get ahead? Dale Carnegie will answer these questions for you, in person on this program every Tuesday night at this same time. You'll be amazed to see how helpful he can be to you. One word you hear on this program may change your whole career – may reveal to you a magic key to the happiness and success which Dale Carnegie has already brought thousands of folks who thank the day they learned his secret of how to win friends and influence people.

(PAUSE FOR COAST SWITCH)

Thousands more thank the day they also discovered the secret of the "friendly" shave. For here, men, is that shave that makes your face feel "friendly" – makes it feel like smiling and winning friends! Here's why! Colgate Rapid Shave Cream is made from a specially created formula that is the scientific secret of true shaving comfort.

Now, Dale Carnegie, in person!

(PAUSE FOR COAST SWITCH)

CARNEGIE

Good Evening, everybody…

GRAUER

Tell me, Dale, how did you discover these rules of yours for getting along with people?

CARNEGIE

My rules? Great Scott! They are not my rules! All I have done is to condense and put into a book the rules that successful men of all ages have used to win friends and influence people.

GRAUER

Why did you write a book on the subject, Dale?

CARNEGIE

Well, Ben, when you find a man who has written a book on dieting, look for a dyspeptic. And when you find a man who has written a book on HOW TO WIN FRIENDS AND INFLUENCE PEOPLE, look for just what you are looking at now – a man who has made so many stupid, blundering, asinine mistakes himself, that finally, in despair, he studies the subject for his own guidance.

GRAUER

Tell me, Dale, just how do you intend to conduct this laboratory of human relations on the air?

CARNEGIE

Well, in order to help people with their problems, I have to know just what those problems are. So I am going to ask everyone listening to this program, and who has some serious problem, to sit down and write to me in care of the National Broadcasting Company, New York City. If your problem is one that we all have to face, I shall invite you to appear on our program.

GRAUER

What's the first problem you're going to tackle, Dale?

CARNEGIE

Suppose I ask you this question, Ben. What is the commonest cause of failure in this world? What would you answer?

GRAUER

The commonest cause for failure? Hmm. Oh – lack of ability.

CARNEGIE

No. The answer is fear! "Fear defeats more men than anything on this earth". And the most terrible kind of fear is the one we call an Inferiority Complex. This not only applies to men and women in business but also in every day social contact – we are afraid to do this, we are afraid to do that.

GRAUER

How about an example, Dale?

CARNEGIE

That's just what I've done. I've invited a person to the studio tonight who has had one of the worst cases of fear, I've ever known. Yet, by proper training, she overcame her fear completely. Everyone knows we men have fears, but unfortunately, it's universal. So, as an example of this, I've invited a young businesswoman to come here tonight... because I think her story will give courage to everyone listening in who suffers from fear. Her name is Miss Olga Giddy and she lives at 123 West 52 Street, New York City. Miss Giddy, step up to the microphone. Miss Giddy, will you tell the audience the state of mind you were in when you first came to me?

GIDDY

Well, as I told you then, Mr. Carnegie, I was so terrified at meeting people that when I saw someone I knew, I'd actually cross to the other side of the street to avoid speaking to them. And I worked nine months in my office without ever having lunch with anyone.

CARNEGIE

And you found, didn't you, that your fear was a tremendous handicap in your work?

GIDDY

A terrific handicap, Mr. Carnegie.

CARNEGIE

Now, Miss Giddy, do you mind if I tell the radio audience what I told you when you came to me with your problem?

GIDDY

Please do, Mr. Carnegie.

CARNEGIE

I explained to Miss Giddy that the only way in the world to conquer fear is to do the very thing that you are afraid to do. I said to her, "Go out and meet people… Seize every opportunity to talk to people", and I warned her that at first it wouldn't be easy.

GIDDY

And believe me, Mr. Carnegie, at first, it wasn't easy! It nearly killed me!

CARNEGIE

But it worked, didn't it?

GIDDY

I'll say it did. Little by little I gained courage, belief, faith in myself and now I'm not afraid to talk to anybody.

CARNEGIE

Believe me, Miss Giddy, the very fact that you are here in front of this microphone, talking to our audience on a coast to coast hookup, proves how thoroughly you have conquered fear. And all of you listening in can do this very same thing that Miss Giddy has done – conquer your fear. And one of the best examples of that I know was proven by one of America's greatest flyers.

Before Col. Charles Lindbergh married Anne Morrow –he was teaching her to fly in Mexico City.

They took off in his plane – and when they got up in the air, they lost a wheel! In landing they had a might narrow escape.

And here's the point! Immediately after that, he not only went up in a plane – he took Anne Morrow with him.

Why?

Because it was the thing they feared to do! Many of you may be afraid to try these rules – and I can't help you, unless you will help yourself. So here's a suggestion:

Each week let's take a "How to Win" rule…a rule that has worked for others in the past.

Now, write this down…it's your "How to Win" rule for this week:

DO THE THING YOU ARE MOST AFRAID TO DO!

For if you don't lick your fears, your fears will lick you! Thank you, Miss Giddy!

How to Get a Raise

Dale Carnegie offers sage advice on the timeless issue of "how to get a raise".

Tune in as Carnegie demonstrates the right way, and the wrong way, of how to get what you want.

© Copyright 2007 – BN Publishing

www.bnpublishing.com

info@bnpublishing.com

ALL RIGHTS RESERVED

Remington Rand

Presents

"HOW TO WIN"

featuring

Dale Carnegie

CAST

Announcer

Dale Carnegie

James Smith

Knox

Smith (D)

ANNOUNCER

Listen – and learn "How to Win".
(OPENING MUSICAL THEME)

ANNOUNCER

Remington Rand presents a new radio program, "How to Win", featuring Dale Carnegie, author of the best-selling book, "How to Win Friends and Influence People". For twenty years, Dale Carnegie's sound, practical advice has been helping people to get ahead, in business and in everyday life. In a moment, we will hear from him. But first, listen to – (BUZZ OF CLOSE SHAVER) (WAIT FOR BUZZ TO STOP) That was the voice of the Remington Rand Close-Shaver – a buzz that will soon be heard in millions of American homes, for a few minutes every morning – and occasionally in the evening.

And here's Dale Carnegie, to tell you how to win success in other things.

CARNEGIE

Greeting, everybody – and welcome to our "How to Win" program.

ANNOUNCER

What's the problem for this evening?

CARNEGIE

It's one that I am sure is bothering thousands of our listeners. I have received hundreds of letters on the same subject. They all ask substantially the same question – "How can I get a raise?" So for this evening's program, I have picked out a representative case – that of James Smith. I have talked with Mr. Smith – and he is standing beside me, here at the microphone. Mr. Smith, why did you write to me?

SMITH

Well, I had heard about what you are doing to help people like me – people who want things and don't know how to get them for themselves.

CARNEGIE

I see.

SMITH

I don't know what to do – but I've got to do something. I worry about money so much that sometimes, I can hardly keep my mind of my office work. I certainly hope you can help me.

CARNEGIE

Perhaps I can. You want a raise.

SMITH

I certainly do! I've got to have one, Mr. Carnegie! I can't get along without it! But my boss is might hard-boiled!

CARNEGIE

I've heard a good many people say that.

SMITH

But Mr. Knox, my boss, really is! He's irritable – he flies off the handle when little things go wrong.

CARNEGIE

Don't forget, Mr. Smith, that your boss has even more to worry about than you have. He has greater responsibilities. He has to worry about his own family, the way you do – and about his whole business family, as well.

SMITH
I know that, Mr. Carnegie. But, well – I need that raise.

CARNEGIE
All right. Now tell me something – do you deserve a raise?

SMITH
I think so.

CARNEGIE

Don't you know?

SMITH

Yes – I do. I'm a bookkeeper. At least, that's my work. But I'm always thinking about the good of the whole business. I've worked out some ideas that Mr. Knox has liked. He's used them.

CARNEGIE

Have you produced a good idea lately and told Mr. Knox about it?

SMITH

Well – no, I guess I've been too worried about trying to make both ends meet.

CARNEGIE

You've already asked your boss for a raise, haven't you?

SMITH

Yes, sir. I told you about that.

CARNEGIE

I know you did – and in a moment, we'll tell the audience about it, and try to find out why you didn't get what you asked for.

SMITH

I didn't get anything! I don't even know whether I've still got a job or not.

CARNEGIE

All right. Now, Mr. Smith, with your permission, I'd like to show our listeners just how you asked for a raise. We have two actors here, who will impersonate you and your boss, Mr. Knox. I want you to listen and see if this is what happened.

SMITH

All right, sir.

CARNEGIE

In the first place, you were thinking of

only one thing – getting a raise from Mr. Knox. So you walked up to the door of his private office – (SOUND OF TYPEWRITER FADES IN, AS CARNEGIE'S VOICE FADES OUT) – and you knocked on the door.

(TYPEWRITER CONTINUES. KNOCK ON THE DOOR)

KNOX
(OFF, CALLING) Come in, come in! (DOOR OPENS AND CLOSES, ON MIKE. TYPEWRITER OUT, AS DOOR CLOSES)

SMITH (D)
Good Morning, Mr. Knox.

KNOX

Huh? Oh – good morning, Smith. Wait a second. I'm trying to find something. (CALLING). Miss Johnson – Miss Johnson! (RUSTLING OF PAPERS) Hang it, that correspondence must be around here somewhere. (CALLING, LOUDER). Miss Johnson! I swear, whenever I need that girl, she's always powdering her nose! And I pay her good money, too! (PHONE BELL RINGS, ON MIKE).

SMITH (D)

Perhaps I can help you find the correspondence.

KNOX

Keep away! I don't want my desk all messed up! I know the stuff is here, someplace. (PHONE BELL RINGS) Doggone that girl! Why doesn't she answer the phone! That's her job, not mine. She gets paid for keeping unimportant people away from me! Wait, now. Ah – here's what I was looking for. I knew it was right here. Now, let me see. Er – what is it you want, Smith? I'm busy – mighty busy. Spit it out and get it over with.

SMITH (D)

Well, sir – you see –

KNOX

I don't see anything – except that you're interrupting me and wasting my time. What is it you want?

SMITH (D)

I – I want a raise, Mr. Knox.

KNOX

You want what?

SMITH (D)

A raise. You see, I've been working here for three years, and –

KNOX

And you're lucky to have had a job that long, the way things have been! Here I'm trying to keep this business going – working night and day to try to break even – and you want a raise!

SMITH (D)

But I think I'm entitled to it, sir.

KNOX

Is that so? Well, Smith, if you think you can make more money some place else, you go right ahead and do it. I've got a hundred applications for jobs in my file – right over there.

SMITH (D)

You don't understand, Mr. Knox.

KNOX

Oh, I understand, all right. You're trying to hold me up. You think I can't get along without you. Well, I can have a dozen bookkeepers in here tomorrow morning who'll be glad to work for half what I'm paying you!

SMITH (D)

Now, Mr. Knox – don't get me wrong. I wasn't thinking about quitting. It's just that I –

KNOX

It's just that you think you can bleed me for more money. I know all about it. Here I've kept you on while business was bad – and you haven't any gratitude. Smith, you're mighty lucky, if you only knew it.

SMITH (D)

Yes, sir. But I really need –

KNOX

What you need more than anything else is your job. Isn't that true?

SMITH (D)

Well – yes, sir.

KNOX

Then go back to your desk and remember that. And remember one other thing – there are lots of other men who want the job you've got.

SMITH (D)

Yes, sir. (DOOR OPENS AND CLOSES)

CARNEGIE

(COMING IN) Well, Mr. Smith, it was pretty bad, wasn't it?

SMITH

It was awful, Mr. Carnegie. And that's just what happened.

CARNEGIE

I'm afraid you made a mess of it – but I believe I can help you. In the first place, you got off to a bad start. You were licked before you asked Mr. Knox anything – and he knew it.

SMITH

I don't see how.

CARNEGIE

Your whole attitude showed it. You were worrying about the fact that you wouldn't get the raise you were going to ask for. And one other thing. If you want to win over a man like Mr. Knox, don't talk to him when he's upset or in a bad mood. He certainly was, when you tackled him.

SMITH

What should I have done, when I found him that way?

CARNEGIE

Did you ever hear of a strategic retreat?

SMITH

Of course. But once I was in his office, it would have been cowardly for me to back out.

CARNEGIE

Not a bit. Do you think Napoleon, Washington or Lee were cowards?

SMITH

No, sir.

CARNEGIE

Well, they won a lot of battles by knowing when not to attack. When you found that Mr. Knox was upset, you could easily have asked him some question about your work and beat a retreat.

SMITH

I can see that now, sir. But that couldn't have been all that was wrong.

CARNEGIE

No, you made one other basic mistake. You ruined your chances the minute you said, "I want a raise".

SMITH

But I did want a raise. I still want one.

CARNEGIE

But Mr. Knox doesn't want you to have one, does he?

SMITH

No.

CARNEGIE

You knew that, before you went into his office. You knew that there was a sharp conflict of "wants" – and yet, the first thing you did was to remind him of it. And then, you actually started to argue with him.

SMITH

I know it. But he was wrong.

CARNEGIE

You didn't convince him of it, did you?

SMITH

No, I didn't.

CARNEGIE

Well, Mr. Smith, there's no use in my going ahead and enlarging on your mistakes. That kind of thing is merely destructive criticism – and I'm trying to give you more help than that – real, constructive help. So let me show you what I would have done, if I had been in your place.

SMITH

I wish you would, Mr. Carnegie. I know it would help me.

CARNEGIE

Remember, now – I'm impersonating you, this time.

SMITH

I understand that.

CARNEGIE

I'm a bookkeeper, working for Mr. Knox – and I want a raise. I feel I'm entitled to one. But I'm not going to try to get one, unless I find him in a pleasant state of mind.

SMITH

I remember that.

CARNEGIE

All right. Well then – here I go, walking up to the door of Mr. Knox's private office. (SOUND OF TYPEWRITER FADES IN) I knock on the door. (SOUND OF KNOCKING)

KNOX

(OFF, CALLING) Come in. Come in. (DOOR OPENS AND CLOSES. SOUND OF TYPEWRITER OUT, AS DOOR CLOSES)

CARNEGIE

Good Morning, Mr. Knox.

KNOX

Oh, it's you, Smith.

CARNEGIE

Yes, sir.

KNOX

Well, what's on your mind? I'm pretty busy, you know.

CARNEGIE

I realize that, sir. With business picking up, we're all of us keeping busy. Mr. Knox, here's a list of accounts I've made up. They're quite a little past due – and they're all good accounts. Some of our best ones are here.

KNOX

That so? Let me see it.

CARNEGIE

Here you are, sir.

KNOX

Hmm. I had no idea that some of our old customers were letting their accounts run up like this. It's bad!

CARNEGIE

That's right, sir. But we can't afford to offend them by going after them through the usual collection channels.

KNOX

Well – have you anything to suggest? We can always use cash.

CARNEGIE

I thought it might be a good idea if I dropped them a note and asked them to pay up. Just a short, formal letter. What do you think?

KNOX

Why should you write them? A lot of them are old business friends of mine.

CARNEGIE

That's why I think I should sign the letters. Then, if any of them get mad, you can blame it on me. Say the letter was just a routine form, sent out by the bookkeeping department.

KNOX

That's not a bad idea, Smith. Go ahead and try it.

CARNEGIE

Thanks. There's something else, too, Mr. Knox.

KNOX

What is it – another idea?

CARNEGIE

Well, yes – in a way. I know how slow business has been for the past few years.

KNOX

It's been worse than that.

CARNEGIE

Yes, sir. And I'm just as glad as you are, to see things improving.

KNOX

That's good, Smith. I like to feel that my employees take a real interest in the business. Yes, things are getting better – a little better, anyway.

CARNEGIE

I knew you'd pull us through, sir.

KNOX

Well, that's nice of you, Smith.

CARNEGIE

I know we're not out of the woods yet, but – well, here's what I mean. One of the reasons this business will keep on going is because you always get your money's worth. You're a good buyer, Mr. Knox.

KNOX

Smith – I'll let you in on a secret. That's the way I built this business – and that's the way I've kept it going. But – what are you getting at?

CARNEGIE

Mr. Knox – no matter what happens, I'll always try to give you the best I've got. I've always done it. But it's pretty hard, sometimes, for me to keep on doing it, because – well, I worry a lot.

KNOX

You worry? What about?

CARNEGIE

Money.

KNOX

Oh! So that's it.

CARNEGIE

Yes, sir. Understand, Mr. Knox – I know I'm lucky to have my job. And of course, I realize that I ought to do my worrying on my own time, and not on yours. But – it's pretty hard to control that sort of thing.

KNOX

Do you really have to worry about money, Smith?

CARNEGIE

Yes, sir. Prices are going up – rents, and everything else. And I've got my family to think about. It isn't just myself.

KNOX

So you want a raise, do you?

CARNEGIE

Well – here's the point. I can do more work for you, and better work, if my mind is at rest. If I can just think about my job and concentrate on it, I know I can do a whole lot more intelligent work. You know how it is yourself, don't you?

KNOX

Yes, I suppose so. But look here, Smith –

CARNEGIE

Pardon me, Mr. Knox. I don't want you to think about it as a raise. Consider that it's an investment you're making in me – an investment from which you can expect more and better work. I know it will be a good one.

KNOX

You do? Well, how big do you think the investment should be, to ease your mind?

CARNEGIE

Not much, sir. Say five dollars a week, to see how it works.

KNOX

Well, I guess that won't break us. I'll think it over, Smith.

CARNEGIE

Thank you, Mr. Knox. I'll get those collection letters out right away.

KNOX

Oh, yes, Here's the list.

CARNEGIE

I've got a copy of it. You can keep that one. I'll check it up with you, when the collections start coming in.

KNOX

I hope they do. And, Smith.

CARNEGIE

Yes, sir.

KNOX

If you don't get that raise within two weeks, you'd better remind me of it.

CARNEGIE

Thank you, sir. (DOOR OPENS AND CLOSES) (SOUND OF TYPEWRITER, AS DOOR OPENS. IT REGISTERS AND FADES OUT)

SMITH

(COMING IN) Mr. Carnegie, that was great! From the way you did it, I can see a whole lot of mistakes I made with Mr. Knox.

CARNEGIE

I thought you would. First of all, when you want a man to say "yes", let him get into the habit of agreeing with you. If he starts saying "yes", it's easier for him than to say "no".

SMITH

And I should have started talking about something else Mr. Knox was interested in – something about the business, instead of about myself.

CARNEGIE

That's right. You should have talked about what he was going to get, instead of what you wanted.

SMITH

I wish I'd known all this, before I talked with him. It might have been different.

CARNEGIE

Well, there's still time. If you've given Mr. Knox some good ideas in the past, he isn't going to fire you. And you can ask his for a raise again, you know. Don't make it too soon. Give him a chance to forget the last time you asked.

SMITH

I certainly will. And the next time, I'll make sure he's feeling good, before I ask him.

CARNEGIE

Let me know how you make out, Mr. Smith.

SMITH

I'll do that, Mr. Carnegie – and thanks a whole lot!

ANNOUNCER

Dale Carnegie, author of the best-selling book, "How to Win Friends and Influence People", has demonstrated one way to ask for a raise – and it certainly sounds like a good one. Every day, Monday through Friday, Remington Rand presents this "How to Win" program, featuring Dale Carnegie. The program discusses business and social problems which are bothering a great many listeners.

Staying Connected to Your Teenager

Do you disapprove of your teenage daughter's boyfriend, and don't know what to do about it? Are you stuck in a job that's taking you "nowhere?" Then you won't want to miss this live radio transcript featuring renowned writer and human nature expert Dale Carnegie.

Tune in as Carnegie offer sound advice to parents and youth on a range of important social issues.

© Copyright 2007 – BN Publishing

www.bnpublishing.com

info@bnpublishing.com

ALL RIGHTS RESERVED

REMINGTON RAND

Presents

"HOW TO WIN"

featuring

DALE CARNEGIE

CAST

ANNOUNCER

DALE CARNEGIE

MRS. LAWSON

MR. LAWSON

MRS. LAWSON (D)

EDWARD MURPHY

MURPHY (D)

DR. THOMAS

ANNOUNCER
Listen – and learn "How to Win".
(OPENING MUSICAL THEME)

ANNOUNCER
Remington Rand presents the new radio program, "How to Win", featuring Dale Carnegie, author of the best-selling book, "How to Win Friends and Influence People". In a moment, we will hear from Dale Carnegie, who has spent twenty years devoted to helping people in all walks of life – helping them to get ahead, in both business and social activities. This evening, he will give a definite, helpful solution to two problems that are troubling many thousands of people.

And here is Dale Carnegie, to tell you – "How to Win".

CARNEGIE
Greeting, everybody – and welcome to another "How to Win" program. We're going to take up two problems this evening – first that of a mother who is worried about her daughter – and second,

that of a young man who is buried in a job which holds out no future. Both these people are here with us. First let me introduce Mrs. Lawson.

MRS. LAWSON
(OFF MIKE) How do you do.

CARNEGIE
A little closer to the microphone, please. That's it. Now then, you and I have talked over your problem – but our listeners don't know anything about it. Will you tell them?

MRS. LAWSON
Of course. My daughter is being flattered by the attentions of the local football hero. He wears nice clothes and is a good dancer. All the girls like him. They're jealous of my youngster. But this young man isn't the kind my husband and I want her to marry.

CARNEGIE
And the matter has become quite a serious situation, hasn't it, Mrs. Lawson?

MRS. LAWSON
It certainly has. It's practically the only thing my husband and I have ever quarreled about.

CARNEGIE
Now, Mrs. Lawson, with your permission, I'd like to give our listeners some idea of how matters stand, the way you explained it to me. We have people here who will impersonate you and your husband.

MRS. LAWSON
You have my permission, of course.

CARNEGIE
Very well. Here, then, is a typical scene in the Lawson household after dinner. Mr. and Mrs. Lawson are seated in the living room. (HIS VOICE BEGINS TO FADE OUT) Mr. Lawson doesn't seem to be very interested in the evening newspaper. (FADE IN SOUND OF NEWSPAPER, AS MR. LAWSON SHAKES IT)

MR. LAWSON
Where's Peggy?

MRS. LAWSON (D)
Up in her room.

MR. LAWSON
Primping, I suppose – getting ready to go out again.

MRS. LAWSON (D)
That's right. There's a dance at the country club tonight.

MR. LAWSON
I suppose she's going with that young scamp of an Ed Forrest.

MRS. LAWSON (D)
(SIGHING) Yes, Henry, she is.

MR. LAWSON
Well, I tell you – I won't stand for it! That boy has only been out of college a year – and he's had three different jobs already! What's more, he's always borrowing money from his friends – I know that for a fact!

MRS. LAWSON (D)
I know he isn't the kind of boy Peggy ought to marry.

MR. LAWSON
You bet he isn't! And if I have anything to say about it, she isn't going to marry him! But she goes out with him every night in the week!

MRS. LAWSON (D)
He's still a football hero, to girls of her age. Don't forget that, Henry.

MR. LAWSON
Playing football in college didn't give that kid anything but a swelled head. I tell you, it's time we forbid Peggy to see him.

MRS. LAWSON (D)
I don't think that's the way to go about it, Henry.

MR. LAWSON
You don't, eh? Well, I'll tell you something. Most of the businessmen I know are beginning to kid me about the nice, ornamental son-in-law I'm going to have. And if you don't do something to make Peggy realize what a nit-wit he is, I'm going to lay down the law to her! (FADING) I won't have it, I tell you!

CARNEGIE
(FADING IN) Well, that's a bad situation, Mrs. Lawson.

MRS. LAWSON
Yes, Mr. Carnegie. That's why I wrote to you about it.

CARNEGIE
Well, I know one thing – and that's what not to do about it. Don't criticize. Don't aggravate the affair by opposing it. That would be the worst thing you could do. If you oppose your daughter, or scold her, or nag her, she's going to want to do just the thing you tell her not to do. In your position – I think I'd try something like this – I would point out to her what good qualities the boy has, BUT – I'd sort of intimate that he is all right as far as he goes. I'd always leave hanging in the air that little word – BUT.

MRS. LAWSON
I'll certainly try it.

CARNEGIE
I would be very friendly with the young man – really friendly. Show your daughter that you like him – but at the same time, act as though he wasn't so

much to get excited about. Try to persuade your husband to do the same. If both of you do that, your daughter is going to have misgivings about the young man, too. She can't help herself. And she won't be in such a hurry to rush off and get married. Right now, your daughter's football hero is all wrapped up in glamour, to her eyes. But time has a way of being a little rough on glamour. Encourage Peggy to make plans for herself – plans, by the way, that aren't connected with marriage. And there's another thing.

MRS. LAWSON
Yes, Mr. Carnegie?

CARENGIE
If you can afford it, take your daughter on a trip – a trip where she may meet men who are even more glamorous and interesting than her football hero. When she does that, she will wake up of her own accord. Try it for one month – and then let me know how it works. I'll be waiting to hear from you, Mrs. Lawson – and good luck!

MRS. LAWSON
Thank you, Mr. Carnegie.

ANNOUNCER
Before Dale Carnegie presents the next problem, the Modern Male Chorus brings us a "College Medley".
(COLLEGE MEDLEY – MALE CHORUS)

ANNOUNCER
It's time for our next problem – and here is Dale Carnegie, to tell you about it.

CARNEGIE
Standing beside me now is a young man named Edward Murphy. Mr. Murphy has a job, but he feels there is no future connected with it. I've talked with him about it, and I hope we can help him out. Mr. Murphy, tell the listeners about your job.

MURPHY
I drive an ambulance. A lot of people may think it's an exciting job, rushing out on emergency calls – ringing the bell and running through red lights. But I don't want to do it all my life.

CARNEGIE
How old are you?

MURPHY
Twenty-nine, sir.

CARNEGIE
Now I want to dramatize for our listeners the talk you had with one of the internees for whom you drive the ambulance. When our actors finish, I want you to tell us whether what they said was right or not.

MURPHY
All right, sir.

CARNEGIE
One night, not so long ago, you were waiting for a call to come in. And you started talking with a new internee, Dr. Thomas. (HIS VOICE STARTS FADING OUT) And you told him –

MURPHY (D)
Of course, I shouldn't bother you with my troubles, Dr. Thomas, but I've been thinking, lately – wondering what I'm going to do, when I get old. They don't keep a man on this job forever.

DR. THOMAS
No – that's right. It takes young men to drive emergency ambulances.

MURPHY (D)
That's the trouble. With you, now, it's different, of course. You won't be riding an ambulance, except for six months. Then you'll go into the hospital and go ahead with your work as a doctor.

DR. THOMAS
Don't forget, Murphy – it's taken me six years of college work to get where I am, and I've got two or three years yet, before I can begin to practice.

MURPHY (D)
I know that. You doctors have a tough time. Yes. But look at me. I don't know anything to do, except drive an ambulance. And I'm twenty-nine. What's going to happen to me?

DR. THOMAS
Can't you get some other kind of a job?

MURPHY (D)
I've never had a chance to study anything. I started to work right out of grammar

school., when I was fourteen.

DR. THOMAS
What hours do you work?

MURPHY (D)
I'm on twenty-four hours, and then off twenty-four hours. I make ninety dollars a month – and there isn't a chance I'll ever make any more. On top of that, I won't even get a pension when they retire me.

DR. THOMAS
Have you any idea what you'd like to do, to get ahead?

MURPHY (D)
You bet I have! I want to go to school and study motors, and dynamos. That's what I'm interested in. But how can I? I've got no money for schooling. I make ninety dollars a month – and I'm married – and there's a baby coming along. I'm stuck, I guess – right where I am.

DR. THOMAS
I'm not so sure about that. Tell me – did you ever hear of Dale Carnegie?

MURPHY (D)
Seems as though I have. Who is he?

DR. THOMAS
He's a man who has helped thousands of people to get ahead – big ones, and little ones, too. I've just finished reading a book of his. Why don't you write to him?

MURPHY (D)
Aw, he don't want to be bothered with guys like me!

DR. THOMAS
Yes, he does. And writing to him won't do any harm. Tell him what you're doing now, and what you want to do. It won't take you long – and it only costs two cents to send a letter.

MURPHY (D)
That's right. (LOUD BELL STARTS RINGING, OFF A BIT. THIS IS A LARGE BELL, CONNECTED WITH A TELEPHONE)

DR. THOMAS
There's another call for us. (FADING OUT). I'll answer the phone.

MURPHY (D)
(CALLING, SLIGHTLY) Right, Doctor! I'll start the motor, (SOUND OF STARTER, MOTOR STARTS, SLOWS

AND IDLES FOR A MOMENT) Was it for us, Doctor?

DR. THOMAS
(COMING IN FAST) Yes! Another automobile accident – Eighth and Broadway.

MURPHY (D)
Eighth and Broadway! I got it!

DR. THOMAS
I'm set!

MURPHY (D)
Here we go! (MOTOR SPEEDS UP. AMBULANCE GONG STARTS, REGISTERS AND FADES)

CARNBEGIE
(FADING IN) Is that what you told Dr. Thomas, Mr. Murphy?

MURPHY
Yes, Mr. Carnegie. And that's how I came to write to you.

CARNEGIE
Well, I've got some news for you. I'll tell you where you can get the kind of a course you want – and it won't cost you a

penny. You may have to buy a textbook or so – but you won't have to pay any money for the course.

MURPHY
That's swell, Mr. Carnegie. When can I start?

CARNEGIE
Two weeks from this coming Monday.

MURPHY
What do I do? I mean, where do I go?

CARNEGIE
You live in Brooklyn.

MURPHY
That's right.

CARNEGIE
Then go to the Brooklyn High School for Special Trades, at 49 Flatbush Avenue Extension, in Brooklyn. Go early in the morning – and register for the WPA course in dynamos and motors. When you finish with that, take other courses along the same line.

MURPHY
You bet I will!

CARNEGIE
Now, here's some advice. Don't merely be content with getting yourself another job. You seem to have plenty of ambition – why don't you try to make yourself a master of motors? Remember that better motors are going to be built in the next twenty years – and if you can figure out a way to do it, you'll make a fortune.

MURPHY
Motors are what I like. I've always liked them – since I was a kid.

CARNEGIE
Fine! Now then – tell me something. Your work driving an ambulance doesn't keep you busy all the time you're on duty, does it?

MURPHY
No, sir.

CARNEGIE
There's another good opportunity for you. Why don't you go to the public library and get a good book on motors and dynamos? Keep it with you on the job.

Then, when you have nothing to do, you can study – for a few minutes, anyway.

MURPHY
I'll do that.

CARNEGIE
That's all. Good luck, my boy – and please let me know how you get along.

MURPHY
I certainly will, Mr. Carnegie. But there's just one other thing.

CARNEGIE
Something else? What is it?

MURPHY
I want to thank you for helping me. I mean it – from the bottom of my heart!

CARNEGIE
Don't thank me. Just help somebody else, when you're in a position to do it.

MURPHY
I'll certainly do that!

BN Publishing

Improving People's Life

www.bnpublishing.com

www.ingramcontent.com/pod-product-compliance
Lightning Source LLC
Chambersburg PA
CBHW032150040426
42449CB00005B/464